For Carter, who always asks
for one more page.
—E.P.

A Joulia Copernicus Book

Copyright © 2019 by Ellie Peterson

Publisher's Cataloging-in-Publication Data

Names: Peterson, Ellie, author.
Title: It's a round , round world! / by Ellie Peterson.
Description: New York, NY: Starberry Books, an imprint of Kane Press, Inc., 2019.
Summary: An intrepid young scientist explains how we know the earth is round.
Identifiers: LCCN 2018965802 | ISBN 9781635921281 (Hardcover) | 9781635921298 (ebook)
Subjects: LCSH Earth (Planet)--Juvenile literature. | Solar system--Juvenile literature. |
Astronomy--Juvenile literature. | CYAC Earth (Planet). | Solar system. | Astronomy. |
BISAC JUVENILE NONFICTION / Science & Nature / Astronomy
Classification: LCC QB631.4 P462 2019 | DDC 525--dc23
Library of Congress Control Number: 2018965802

10 9 8 7 6 5 4 3 2 1

First published in the United States of America in 2019 by StarBerry Books,
an imprint of Kane Press, Inc.

Printed in China

StarBerry Books is a registered trademark of Kane Press, Inc.

Book Design: Elynn Cohen

Visit us online at www.kanepress.com

 Like us on Facebook facebook.com/kanepress

Follow us on Twitter @KanePress

It's a Round, Round World!

Sure looks flat from here.

WRITTEN AND ILLUSTRATED BY
Ellie Peterson

 StarBerry BOOKS

What would happen if you tried to walk to the edge of the earth? Would you find it?

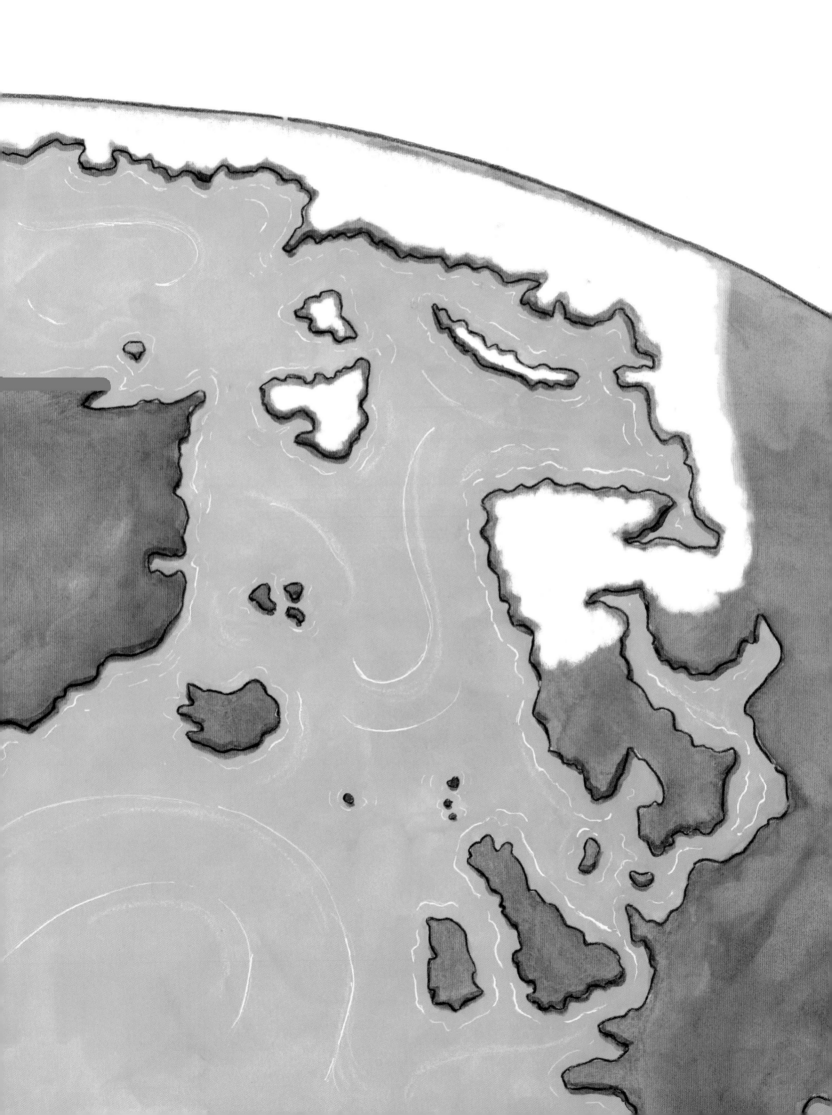

Of course not! Our planet Earth isn't flat.

IT'S ROUND!

I know that, you know that, *everybody* knows that! But have you ever wondered HOW we know the earth is round?

Some people will tell you that Christopher Columbus proved Earth is round.

WRONG!

When he sailed the ocean blue in 1492, Columbus already knew the earth was round. (Actually, most people knew the earth was round back then.)

Columbus was actually looking for a shorter route to Asia, but that's a whole other story. . . .

Ancient Greek, Islamic, and Indian scholars theorized that Earth was round WAY before Columbus's time.

SANTA MARIA

Sailors like Columbus didn't have the scientific equipment we have today. But he and his crew could tell Earth was round from their very own ships.

HOW?

People who lived long before Columbus noticed that when ships sail away from you, they seem to disappear from the bottom. When they sail toward you, they appear from the top.

On a flat Earth, you'd see the entire ship the entire time.

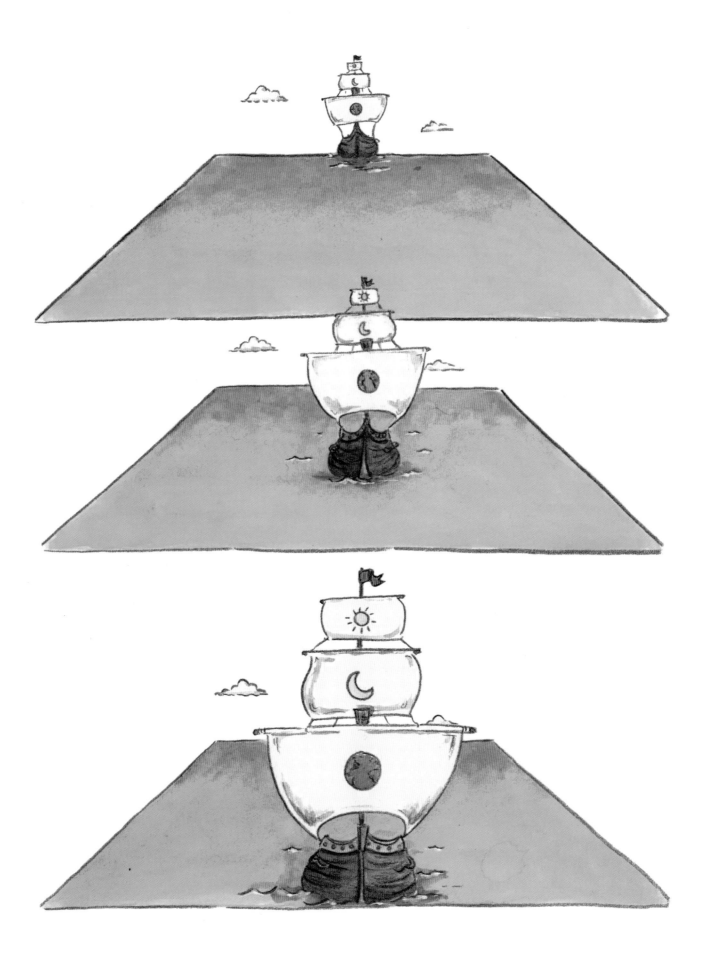

Not only that, but the crow's nest of a ship is only useful if Earth is round.

A crow's nest is a lookout point at the top of a mast.

Are we there yet?!

Being higher up allows you to see farther over the curve of the earth.

On a flat Earth, you'd see the same thing whether you were high or low.

If you don't have a crow's nest handy, another way to prove the earth is round is by viewing a lunar eclipse.

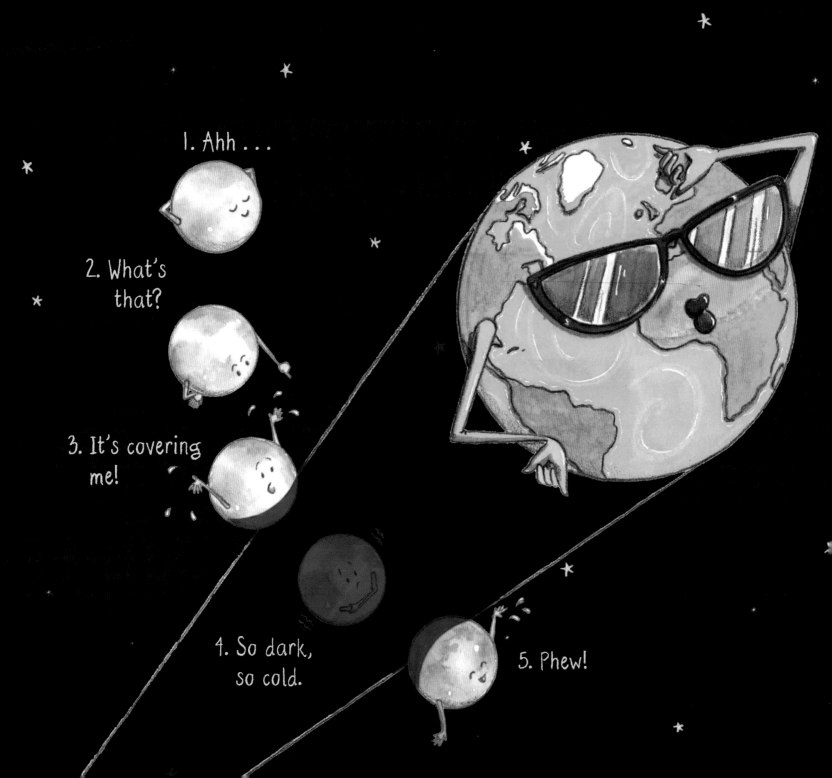

The sun is HUGE! It would take 1.3 million Earths to fill it up.

Do you know what else the sun is?

ROUND!

The earth casts a shadow just like your body does on a sunny day. *Your* shadow appears on the ground, but the *earth's* shadow extends into outer space. If the moon moves into that shadow, it's called a lunar eclipse.

During a lunar eclipse, you can see the shape of Earth's shadow on the moon.

Can we start howling now?

The shape of that shadow is . . .

ROUND!

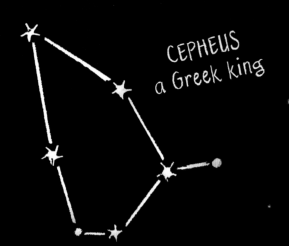
CEPHEUS
a Greek king

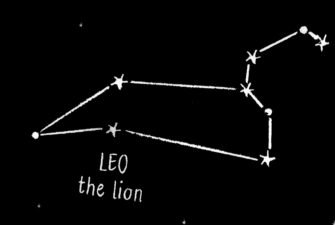
LEO
the lion

ORION
the hunter

Another way to prove Earth is round is by comparing constellations.

People living on the bottom half of the earth (the Southern Hemisphere) see different constellations than people living on the top half (the Northern Hemisphere). That's because they're each looking at a different part of the sky.

CAPRICORN
the goat

Constellations are imaginary pictures in the sky formed by groups of stars.

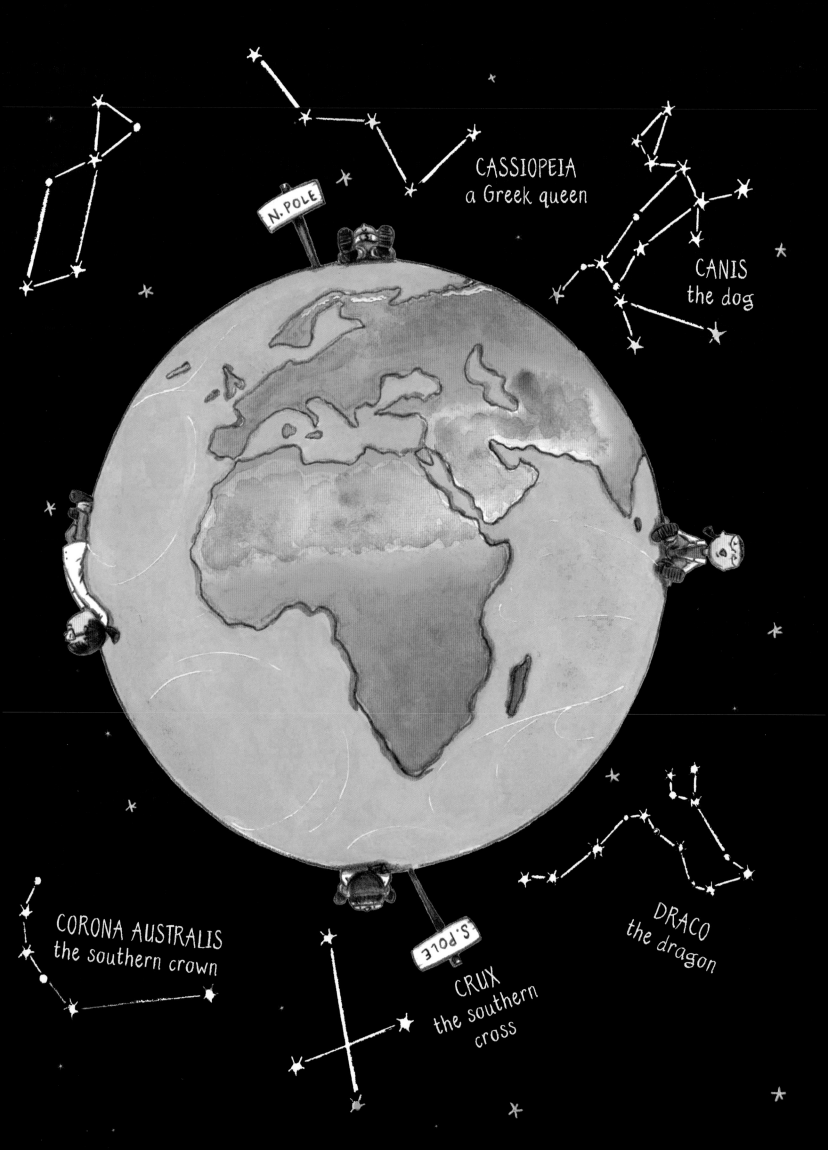

CASSIOPEIA
a Greek queen

CANIS
the dog

N. POLE

CORONA AUSTRALIS
the southern crown

S. POLE

CRUX
the southern
cross

DRACO
the dragon

If Earth were flat, we'd all see the same constellations.

The Big Dipper is also called Ursa Major, which means Great Bear.

* sigh *
the Big Dipper . . .
again?

ONE SIDE
POLE

But we don't need a view of outer space to tell that Earth is round.

That's supposed to be a bear?

OTHER SIDE POLE

How would we explain day and night if Earth were flat?
Everyone in the world would have daytime and nighttime
at the same time!

That's not the case, though. Since our round Earth spins
on an axis, some people have day while others have night.

ZzzZZZ

Earth spins on its axis once each day. This is called a ROTATION.

Earth travels around the sun once each year. This is called a REVOLUTION.

People who live east of us see the sun come up earlier. People who live west of us see the sun come up later.

Scientists divided the earth into time zones. A time zone map helps people figure out the time difference between two areas and helps them set their clocks.

Unfortunately, not everyone checks their clocks.

IN SEATTLE

Oh, Jouly-bean
How is Grandma's
girl doing?

IN NEW YORK

Grandma . . . It's 11 o'clock at night. . . .

Today, most people know the earth is round because we've seen pictures of it that were taken from outer space!

In 1972, astronauts aboard Apollo 17 took the first photo of the ENTIRE Earth from outer space. This picture is called "The Blue Marble."

"The Blue Marble" is the most famous picture of Earth EVER taken.

We also have pictures of all the OTHER planets in the solar system.

Venus? Round.

Mercury? Round.

Did you know that in outer space sunlight is white, not yellow? It's the earth's atmosphere that causes sunlight to appear yellow to us!

If all the other planets in our solar system are round, we can reason that Earth is round too!

Jupiter? You guessed it. Round.

Saturn? Round-diddly-ound!

The more we explore our solar system, the more we learn about this planet we call home.

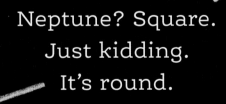

Uranus? Round.

Neptune? Square.
Just kidding.
It's round.

Sometimes, a fact is repeated so often (like Earth being round), that we take it for granted. We never stop to wonder HOW we know it.

The good thing is that you can almost always figure out HOW by making careful observations of the world around you!

WHAT ELSE DO YOU THINK YOU KNOW?

HOW TO BE A SCIENTIST

More than likely, you've never bothered to question Earth's round shape. I'll bet you can't even remember a time when you didn't think the earth was round! We just *know*, don't we?

Knowing that the earth is a sphere (not a perfect sphere, mind you—it bulges a bit in the middle) helps us understand many scientific concepts. The seasons, for instance. Or eclipses. Or the cause of day and night. And don't forget gravitational force! And Earth's magnetic field! The shape of our planet is the key to unlocking SO MUCH SCIENCE.

But you don't need to travel around the globe or blast into outer space to understand Earth's shape.

TRY THIS!

What you'll need:
- a large ball
- a piece of cardboard
- a small figurine or toy

Remember the illustrations of ships that sailed on round and flat versions of the earth? You can model the same concept!

Hold the ball in front of you at eye level. Now hold your toy at the back of the ball, and slide it up over the top and toward you. You will notice that the first thing you see is the top of the toy. As it moves closer to you, more of it will appear, just like ships at sea. This proves that Earth is round!

Next, hold the piece of cardboard in front of you at eye level. Hold the toy at the far end of the cardboard. Then slide the toy closer to you. You will see the entire toy the entire time. It will just appear larger as it gets closer to your eyes. This is not how we see objects move on the surface of the earth, so this proves that Earth is not flat.

TRY THIS, TOO!

What you'll need:
- an area outside with a tall play structure

You can also demonstrate why a crow's nest helps sailors spot land, as shown in the illustrations. Find an area outside where you can see far into the distance at the horizon. First, look into the distance from the ground. Then climb a tall play structure and look in the same direction. You should be able to see farther from a higher position. If Earth were flat, you'd see the same view no matter how high you were.

Remember to have fun experimenting, and never stop questioning what you THINK you know!